Untangling my Mind

Bethany Harewood

BookLeaf Publishing

India | USA | UK

Presentation by *BookLeaf Publishing*

Web: www.bookleafpub.com

E-mail: info@bookleafpub.com

ISBN: 9789358314625

First edition 2023

*This book is dedicated to my Husband, who
without, I would surely not be here.*

ACKNOWLEDGEMENT

I would like to thank my family and friends, for always supporting me, and turning the light on when I was suffocated by darkness.

I would like to thank my Husband, who inspired me to write this and will always be my biggest fan.

I would finally like to thank bookleaf publishing for publishing this book.

PREFACE

She sits, waiting for inspiration to strike,
Her body grows cold,
Her eyes grow weary,
Her legs go numb,
And she decides,
Inspiration has failed to show one too many
times.

So she leaves, and she searches for it herself.

A Poem for my Husband

Although unbeknownst to me,
Each day was spent in search of you,
Now that I have found you,
May our souls forever interlace.

May our branches intertwine,
Our leaves caress in perfect rhyme,
Let there be ample room to grow,
So our roots meet, yet never slow.

Unfinished Symphony

My hobbies often left demolished,
Obsessions, goals,
Left forever unpolished.

Vultures constantly tracking me,
From eager greed, they do not shy.
Waiting to lick up the scraps,
I continue to leave from my unfinished life.

To accentuate, I might,
Just end without finishing this li

Desperate Cravings

The pain inside my chest,
The screaming in my head,
All of this for a simple loaf of bread.

The sweat against my skin,
The paranoia kicking in,
All of this for a bottle of gin.

The knot inside my stomach,
The world begins to plummet,
All of this for a cheap tub of summat.

The shaking in my hands,
I can barely even stand,
All of this for a meal so bland.

My anxiety full swing,
Giving up before I begin,
All of this to lob it in the bin.

Lost Royalty

My blue dress became my Princess dress,
The fabric graced my skin, royalty my desire,
Blue lace, so light,
White bow, still bright,
Oh, it was such a beautiful attire.

Whilst I was robed,
I tore through woods,
Explored high trees,
I launched from swings,
And paddled in streams,
I could conquer all, in my blue dress.

One day, the dress did not fit,
My growing body was against me,
Innocence stolen by the hands of time,
Into a bag, my dress confined.

The prince failed to find me in haste,
I took off my crown, a memory misplaced.
I no longer conversed with mice or birds,
My thrown abandoned, my voice unheard.

The Realm of Serenity

In the realm of dreams, where reality fades,
The girl sits contently, in the world her brain
made.

Where fragments of time tremble at her step,
No new concepts dare breathe without her
permission,
Swaying in the breeze, then molding into
submission.

Only the chosen may enter her world.
Memories of those she trusted,
Turned to marble, delicate and swirled.

She spends her days counting down until she can
return,
The world her brain made, impatiently waiting
for her.
She's the one in control,
Unlike when she wakes,
Soon to spend eternity,
in the world her brain creates.

Whispers of Solace

Underneath the moon's gentle glow,
Life emerges from dens below.
They snuffle and search, finding their supper,
Feeding their young, making soft, gentle rustles.

Amidst this beauty, my mind starts to fray,
Slowly crumbling, thoughts in disarray.
But in the presence of nature's childish grace,
I find peace, if only fleetingly, lost in this place.

Playground of Emotions

The swing set rocks back and forth,
Tempting me to sit down.
But once I am upon it,
It hurls me uncontrollably,
Swinging too high,
Dropping far too low.

When the swing has me high in the air,
I feel invincible,
Knowing if I were to jump, I would surely fly.
But in an instant, it soars back to the ground,
My feet scrape against the tarmac,
My fingers turn white gripping the metal chains,
My string insides twist into knots.

I'm left begging for it to be over,
Longing for the journey between highs and
lows,
To last a little longer.

Resolutions

The beginning of a year, not yet started.
The leaves not yet auburn,
The first murmurs of snow have not yet been
spoken.

Untied to tradition, I chant my resolutions early.

I want to take pride in my choices,
I want to be guided by honest voices,
I want to borrow a moment from each day,
To dust the ever begging cobwebs away.
Make note of contentment, however small.
Bask in the force of the rain,
Open my window to the storm,
Embrace the heat,
Thank the cool.

I want to feel encouraged when staring out the
window,
I want less time spent on ruining the view.

42 Cobbam St.

42 Cobbam Street does not welcome you,
Uninvited, you tread on its ground anew.
Every detail of it carefully designed,
To make you turn away, leave it behind.

Weeds grow high, like a child stretching up,
The warnings of a guard dog, from a sign in the
mud,
The stench of mold wafts from the unstable
structure,
Broken steps to the door, any moment they'd
rupture.

The doorknob, broken, a sharp threat uninvited,
You were begged to turn back from the moment
you were sighted,
To reconsider, steal an alternate view,
For none of this compares to what awaits for
you.

A being stands by the window's frame watching,
Patiently waiting for you to come knocking,
Unsettling presence, not one of this world,
As this house tries to warn you,
Your blood it shall smell.

Unquenchable Flames

I hope the light of my day,
Shall burn on through the night.

I hope I am not remembered as being
a gentle, passive thing,
I hope I am described as spirited, adventurous,
wild,
I hope the fire burning inside of me sets alight to
all I touch,
I hope I explode into a million fireworks on my
way out.

I hope I cause a storm,
Lightening charging through a clear cut night,
I hope those who mourn me don't sit by a
graveside,
But think of me when their legs ache from
running too far.

When they have sand in their shoes,
When they reach the top of the mountain,
I hope I am thought of when Adrenalin is
spiked, When sweat soaks through clothes,
When emotions meet their height.

I hope I don't go quietly,
I hope I don't fizzle and burn out,
I hope I am not a match,
Which was quickly blown back out.

I hope the light of my stay,
Will spark flames once I've left.

A Poem for my Puppy

She bounds straight to me,
A being so wild, tracking through space,
The spirit of one who is free,
Her tail wagging a joyful embrace.

Her whole body vibrates with energy,
A symphony of pure delight,
She stares at me so tenderly,
In her presence, everything feels right.

With every wag of her tail,
To snuggles on an armchair,
Her love and loyalty never fail,
A bond beyond compare.

In her eyes, I see a reflection,
Of the purest love and devotion,
Together, we create a connection,
A bond so full of emotion.

Empty House

My anxiety began like a paper cut,
A tiny tear in the corner of my mind.
Feeding on insecurities and doubt,
Ever growing, strengthening in silence.

Until she grew massive, a chaotic mess,
Bleeding through the plaster I contained her
with.
Soaking into every inch of my head,
Leaving me trembling, forgetting how to tread.

My anxiety is a fire, igniting my core,
Slithering across my skin, heating the tips of my
ears,
Inside my head, she whispers and sears,
Doubt infiltrates, fueling my fears.

I can trust no one, she whispers at night's
embrace,
Hugging me from within, leaving no space.
"You shall always need me," her voice insists,
Manipulating my thoughts, her snarls persist.

I'm driven to madness, longing to trust,
But she convinces me it's all a game, unjust.

I feel sick.

Triggered.

Questioning everyone I once believed in.
Something has happened, I just don't know it
yet,
I know you've betrayed me, I know you're a liar,
You'll leave me, you're exhausted, we're both so
tired.

I'm a walking time bomb, ready to explode,
The darkness within me, will take you down too
when I go.
I plead with you,
I'm fine,
I'm fine,
But deep, deep down, I know I'm confined.

I must take responsibility for my flaws,
But how can I, when she's the cause?
Isolating me from friends, she begs me not to go,
And I almost feel sorry for her then,
Dare I leave her in the house, alone?

I stare at these walls, days upon days,
Doing nothing at all except wishing her away.

But she remains, and you can't help me until I
help myself,
But what if she leaves, and I become the empty
house.

Call from the Depths

"Can you hear that?" becomes my recurring
query,
Joined by "Did you say my name?" so eerie.
They enjoy deceiving, messing with my mind,
People don't understand, leaving me confined.

I hear them, though others remain unaware,
I sound like a madman, caught in their glare.
Whispers in the breeze or shouts so near,
Inches from my face, their presence I hear.

I can almost feel their breath upon my skin,
Their existence, a haunting, deep from within.

Eaten Alive

Fire's cruel embrace,
Swallowing those forgotten,
Can you hear the screams?

Hello, I'm in Crisis

Things helpers have said,
"Go for a walk," they kindly suggest
But on that walk, I have to beg my feet,
To avoid stepping where danger may greet.

"Have a cup of tea," they tell me next,
So I'll plead with my hands, lest
They pour boiling water onto my skin,
Trembling, I'm fighting the urge from within.

"Have a nice soak in the bath," they say,
Yet I'll plead with my head, I'll have to pray,
Not to linger too long beneath the water's charm,
To resist the urge to become one with the bath.

I'll plead with my fingers, the hot tap to control,
To not let it run, consuming my soul.
And my eyes, I'll beg them not to stare,
At my body, filled with self-loathing despair.

Thank you, helpers, for your advice,
But it hasn't brought the desired rest bite.

A Poem for my Sister

Do not let this world consume you,
It's cruelty and coldness, don't let it undo you.

Look both ways, before you tred.
On the darkest of nights, go to bed.
Seek not just happiness, but contentment too,
Search for reality, and keep shining through.

Nature's True Love

Amongst the branches,
She waits, nest made hastily,
Love's creation late.

Peace in Pieces

21

May your struggles no longer define you,
May the light of the morn surely guide you,
May the chains you adorned no longer bind you,
May inner peace hastily find you,

From promises carelessly broken,
From gestures no more than a token,
From wounds that were viscously opened,
From apologies left so often unspoken.

Chaos and Comfort

In the midst of chaos,
I am slowly recovering.
I take note in the quickening rain drops,
Of a mental uncovering.

Her storm flipped our house,
Our lives upside down,
Invariably bursting with gauss,
But stable feet on the ground.

Our own four legged tornado,
Disrobed of her halo,
Her bark bellows, but faux,
Hints of a rainbow's sweet glow.

She's my personal panacea,
No longer calling mamma mia.

I can see the grace in her,
Perpetually amazed with her.

Dear Future Beth

Wow, you made it,
Well I don't know if you made it but you're
reading this and still alive,
So that is something.

How is the dog?
Did you survive the puppy stage?
How is our family?
Everyone still okay?

You may think you're undeserving,
Of great things,
I hope you find them anyway.

You probably still think that,
Everything is about to go wrong,
And come crashing down,
But you'll catch the spinning plates,
Before they hit the ground.
You always have.

Can I tell you a secret?
I never wanted to be you,
I'm sorry that's mean,
You're probably very cool.

I just had no desire to meet you,
I couldn't begin to understand,
Who you would be.
But now you are here,
And I am you and you are me,
And I hope you're everything,
You currently want to be.

I'm not going to set you tasks,
Goals to complete,
Why do I look at the versions of myself,
And want them to compete?
If you are still here,
Chest still rising and falls,
Then you've done it, babe.
You've completed it all.

I can't believe,
That future me will have a future me,
Because my future seems so unclear,
The ground still so unsteady.
But in this future,
I pray you're still striving,
So that future me's future me,
Is finally thriving.

Darkness to Discovery

Blanket of darkness,
I ignited the light,
Only a flicker, barely yet bright.
A slimmer of hope,
A dream barely dreamt,
An untying of rope,
Tears finally wept.

Out the watery depths,
Finally a breath,
The ocean, rung out my hair,
A goodbye to salt air.

No more salt splattered wounds,
No need fighting old feuds,
The taste of a kiss,
The smell of fresh clothes
No more blood on my lips,
No longer fumes in my nose.

Emotions finally recognised,
A tidying of my fragile mind,
Hoovering up the gloomy thoughts,
An explorer of myself, an astronaut.

www.ingramcontent.com/pod-product-compliance
Lightning Source LLC
LaVergne TN
LVHW021345200726

843509LV00014B/2669